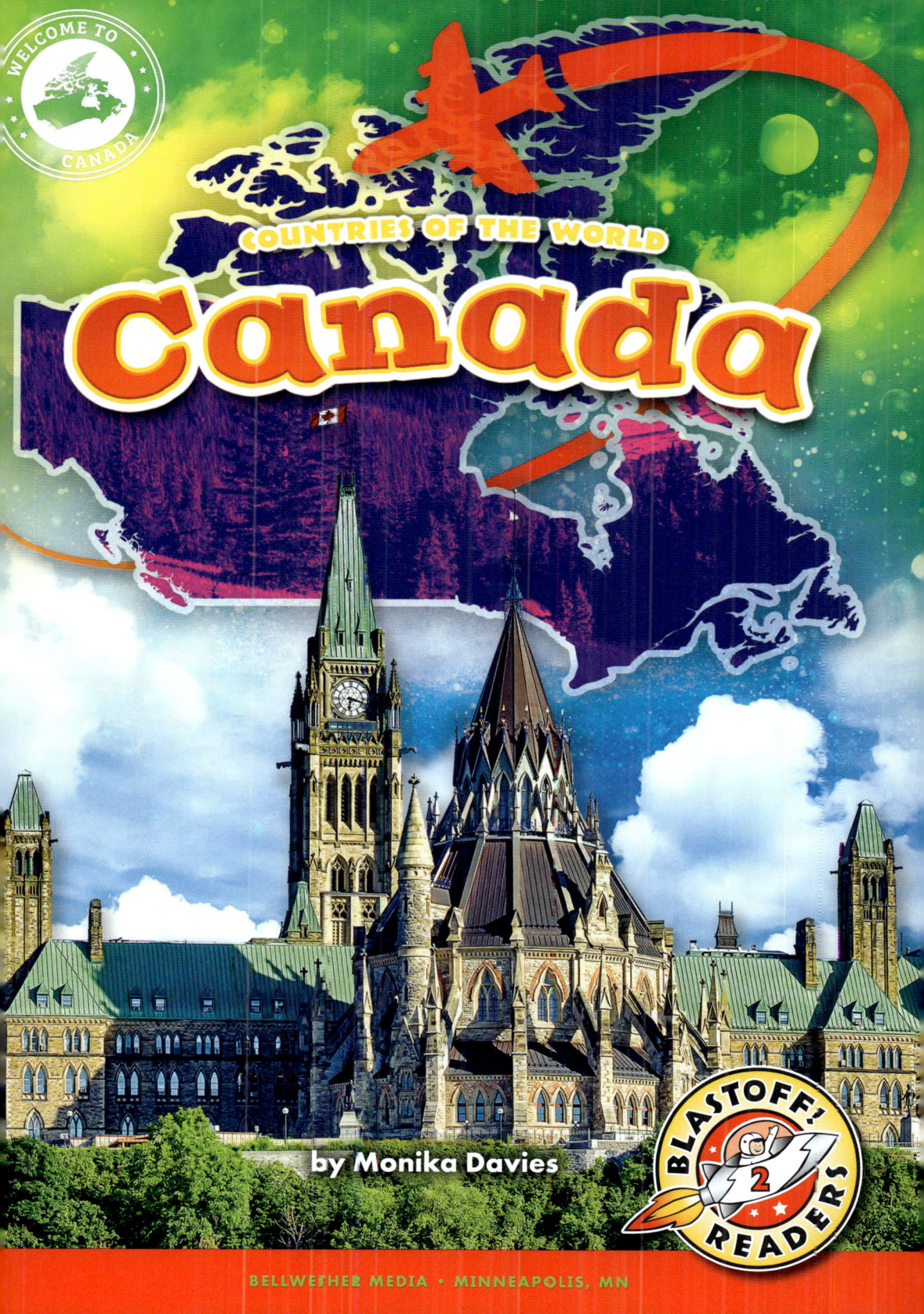

Blastoff! Readers are carefully developed by literacy experts to build reading stamina and move students toward fluency by combining standards-based content with developmentally appropriate text.

Level 1 provides the most support through repetition of high-frequency words, light text, predictable sentence patterns, and strong visual support.

Level 2 offers early readers a bit more challenge through varied sentences, increased text load, and text-supportive special features.

Level 3 advances early-fluent readers toward fluency through increased text load, less reliance on photos, advancing concepts, longer sentences, and more complex special features.

★ **Blastoff! Universe**

This edition first published in 2023 by Bellwether Media, Inc.

No part of this publication may be reproduced in whole or in part without written permission of the publisher. For information regarding permission, write to Bellwether Media, Inc., Attention: Permissions Department, 6012 Blue Circle Drive, Minnetonka, MN 55343.

Library of Congress Cataloging-in-Publication Data

Names: Davies, Monika, author.
Title: Canada / by Monika Davies.
Description: Minneapolis, MN : Bellwether Media, Inc., 2023. | Series: Blastoff! Readers : countries of the world | Includes bibliographical references and index. | Audience: Ages 5-8 | Audience: Grades 2-3 | Summary: "Relevant images match informative text in this introduction to Canada. Intended for students in kindergarten through third grade"– Provided by publisher.
Identifiers: LCCN 2022018225 (print) | LCCN 2022018226 (ebook) | ISBN 9781644877159 (library binding) | ISBN 9781648347610 (ebook)
Subjects: LCSH: Canada–Juvenile literature.
Classification: LCC F1008.2 .D375 2023 (print) | LCC F1008.2 (ebook) | DDC 971–dc23/eng/20220415
LC record available at https://lccn.loc.gov/2022018225
LC ebook record available at https://lccn.loc.gov/2022018226

Text copyright © 2023 by Bellwether Media, Inc. BLASTOFF! READERS and associated logos are trademarks and/or registered trademarks of Bellwether Media, Inc.

Editor: Elizabeth Neuenfeldt   Designer: Gabriel Hilger

Printed in the United States of America, North Mankato, MN.

Table of Contents

All About Canada	4
Land and Animals	6
Life in Canada	12
Canada Facts	20
Glossary	22
To Learn More	23
Index	24

All About Canada

Ottawa

Canada is a huge country. It is the second largest in the world!

Canada is in North America. Its capital is Ottawa.

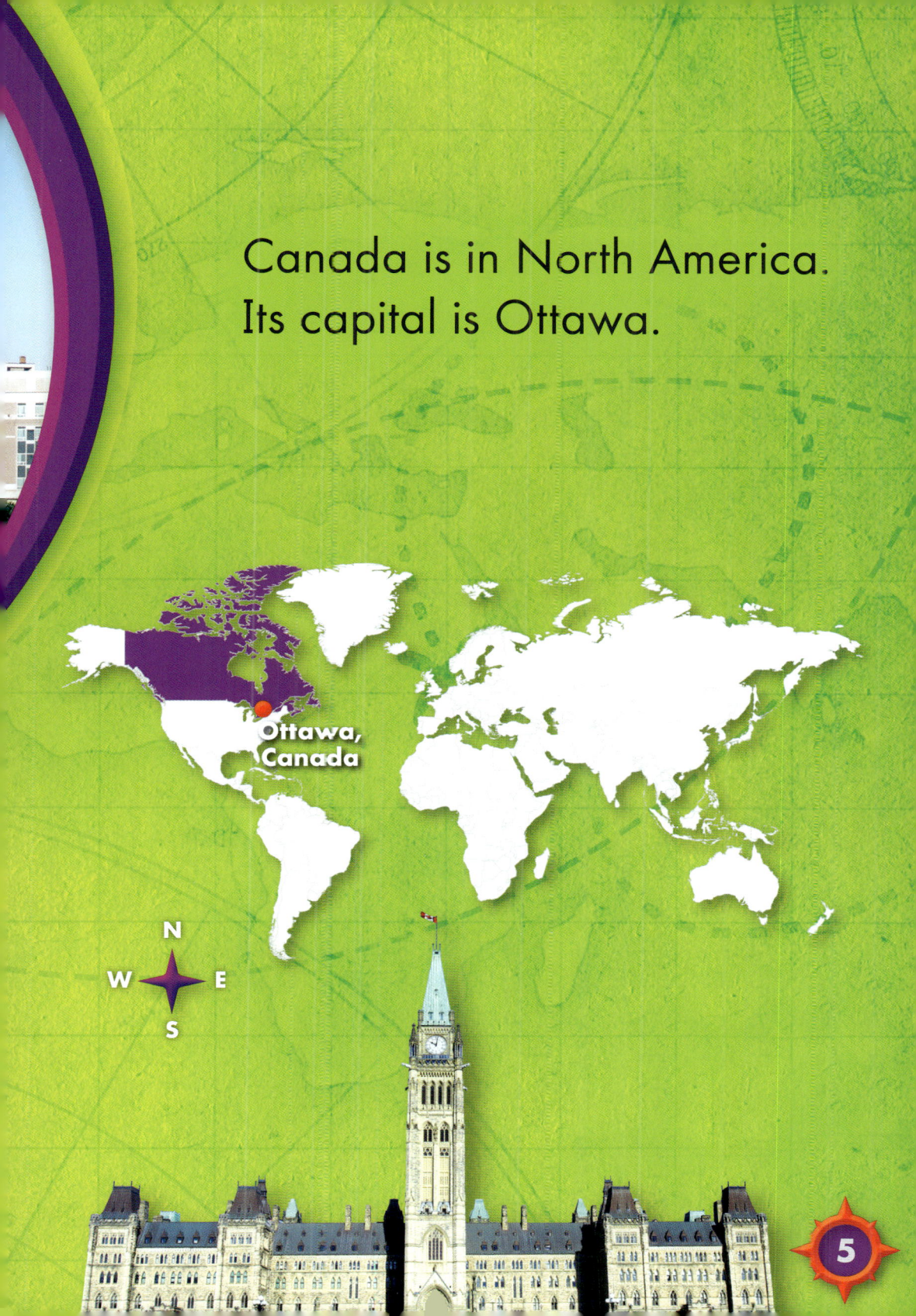

Land and Animals

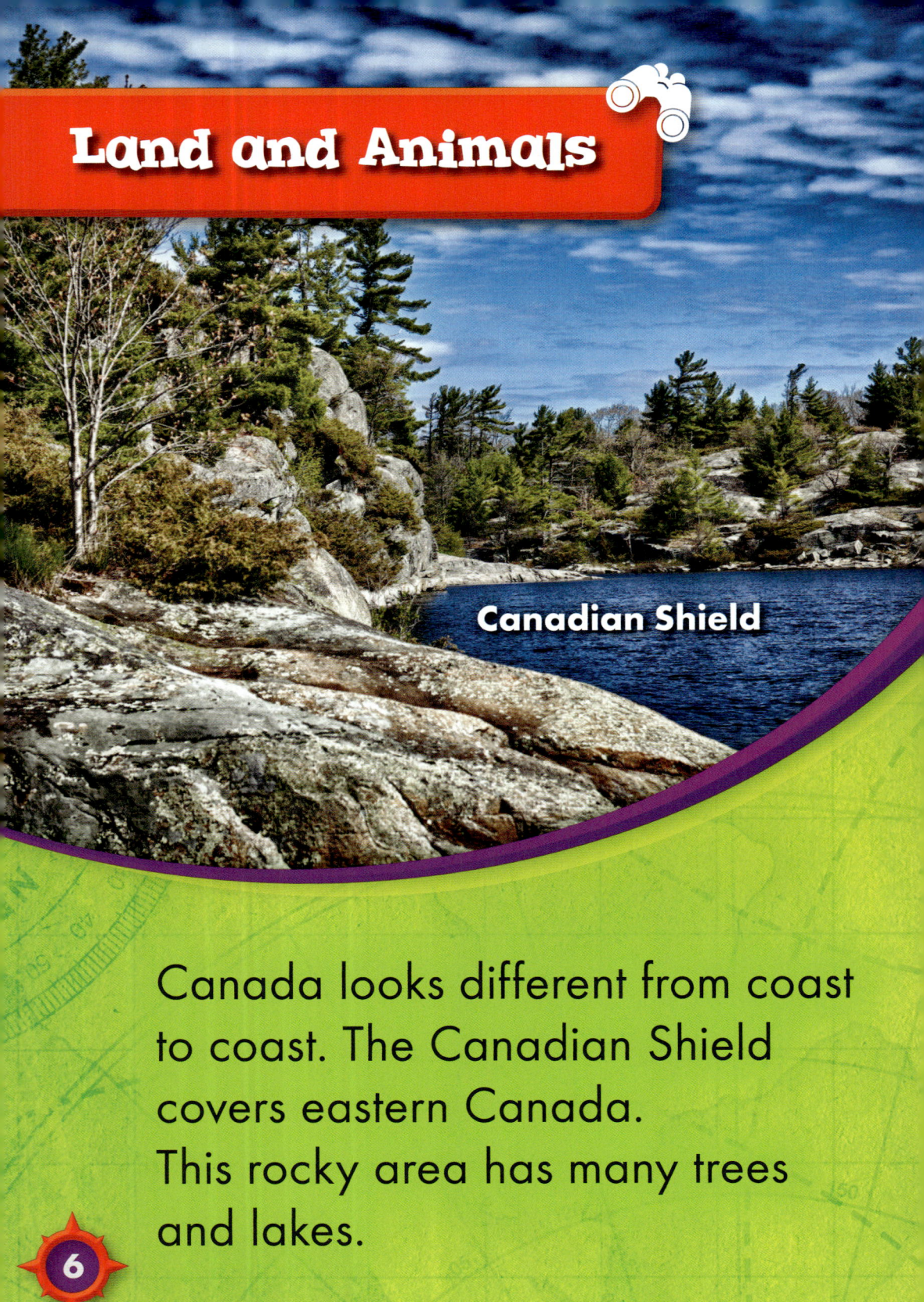

Canadian Shield

Canada looks different from coast to coast. The Canadian Shield covers eastern Canada. This rocky area has many trees and lakes.

Flat, grassy **plains** lie in central Canada.

plains

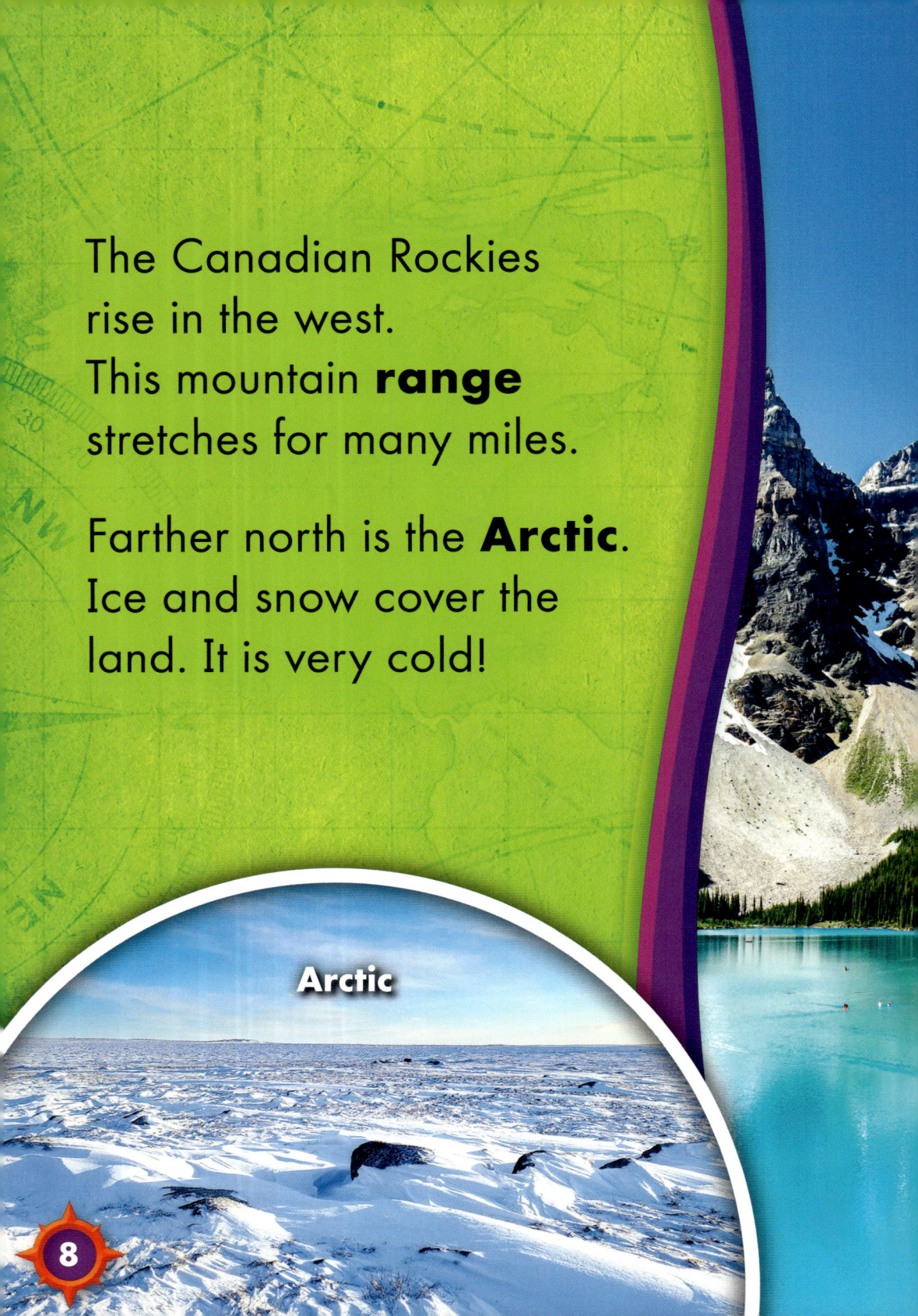

The Canadian Rockies rise in the west. This mountain **range** stretches for many miles.

Farther north is the **Arctic**. Ice and snow cover the land. It is very cold!

Arctic

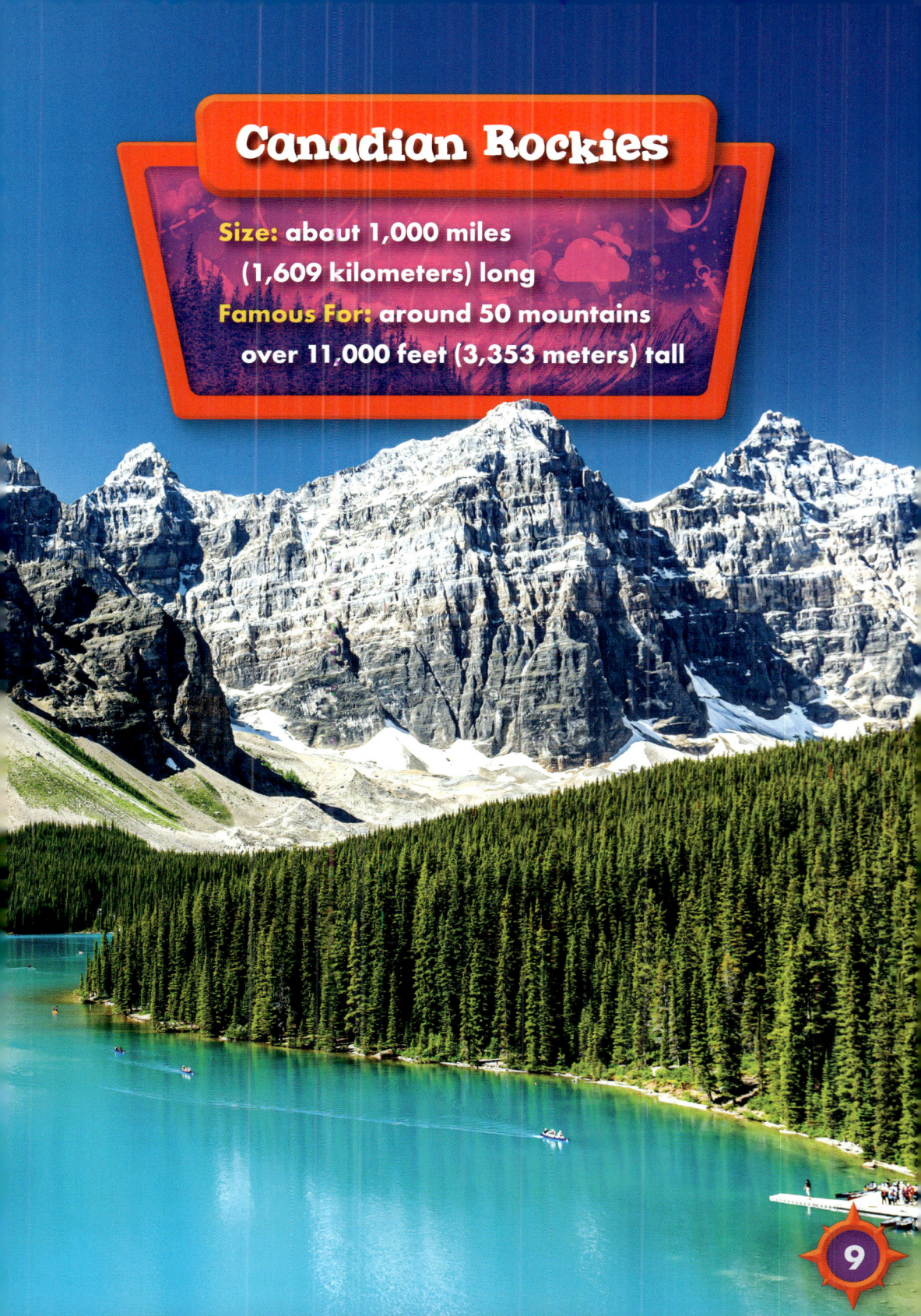

Canadian Rockies

Size: about 1,000 miles (1,609 kilometers) long
Famous For: around 50 mountains over 11,000 feet (3,353 meters) tall

Many animals live in Canada. Moose and black bears **wander** across the country.

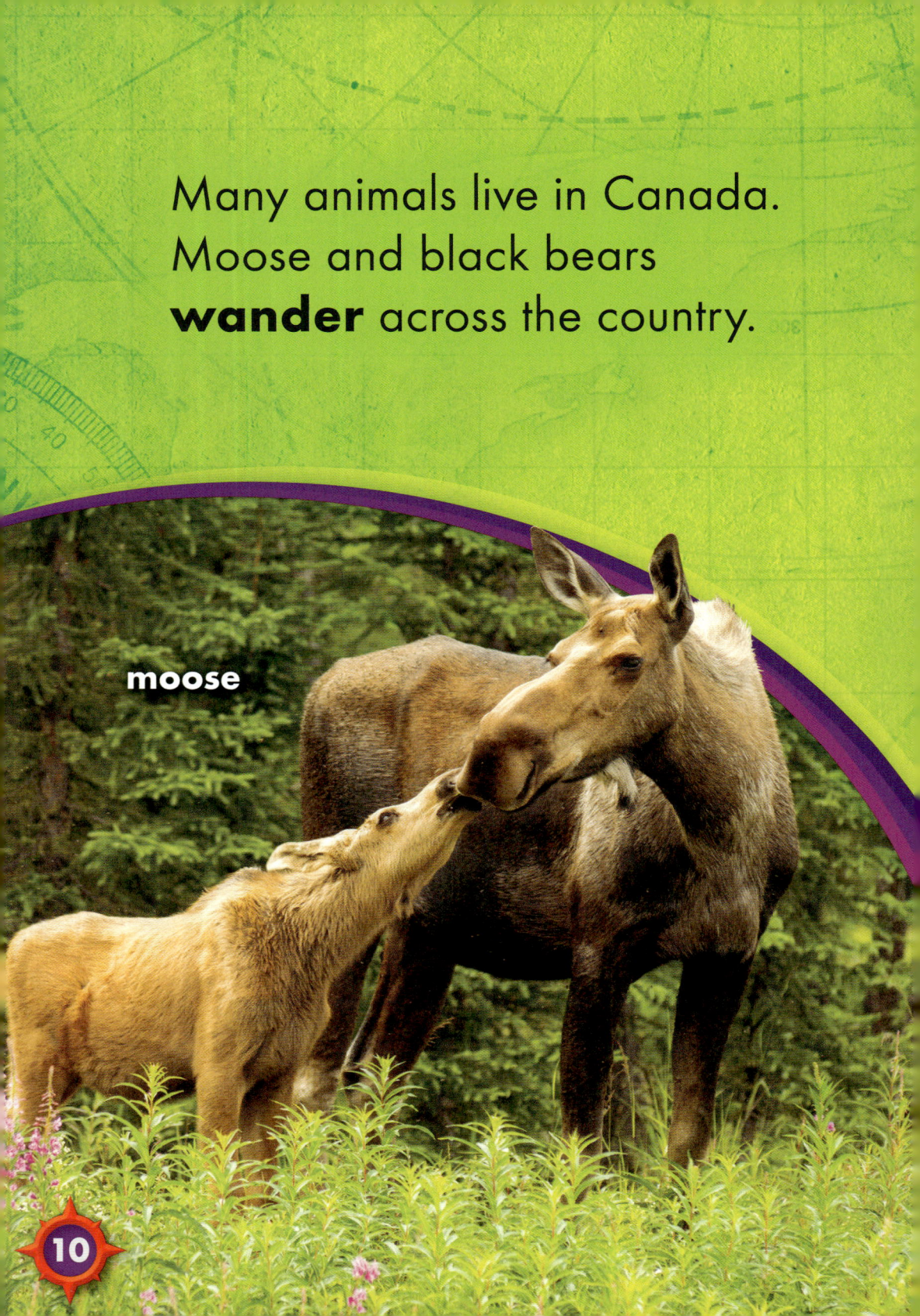

moose

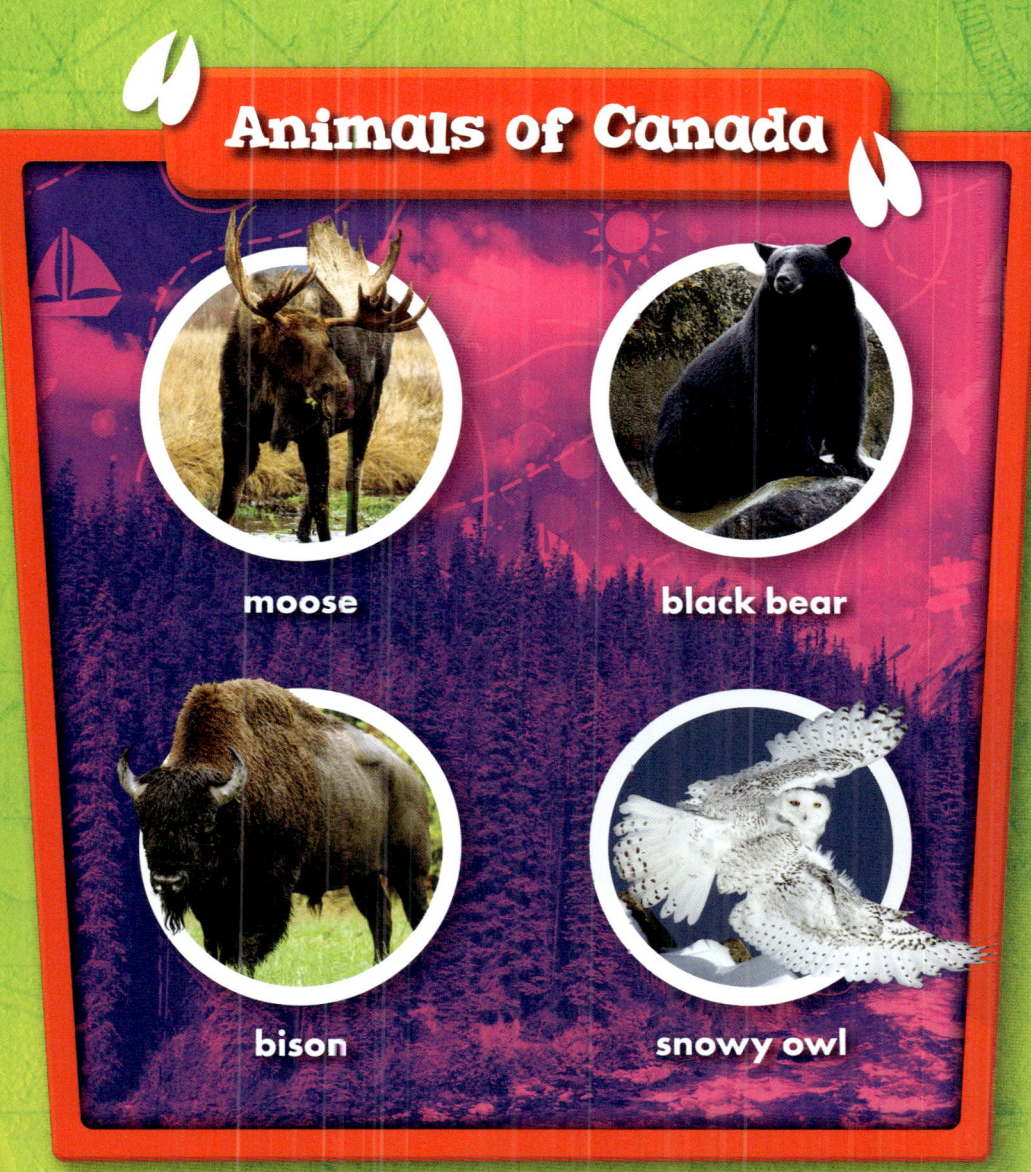

Animals of Canada: moose, black bear, bison, snowy owl

Bison **graze** on the plains. Snowy owls fly above the Arctic.

Life in Canada

Canada is made up of many **cultures**. People may have European backgrounds or Asian backgrounds. Many Canadians speak English or French.

Most Canadians live in cities. Toronto has the largest **population**.

Toronto

canoeing

curling

Canadians enjoy many activities. Some like canoeing. Others enjoy **curling** or downhill skiing.

Hockey is a popular sport. Fans cheer for their favorite teams!

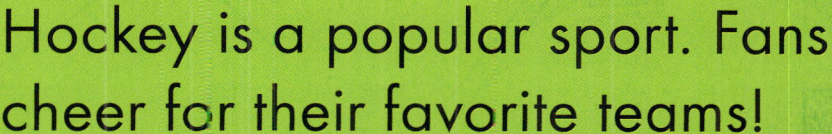

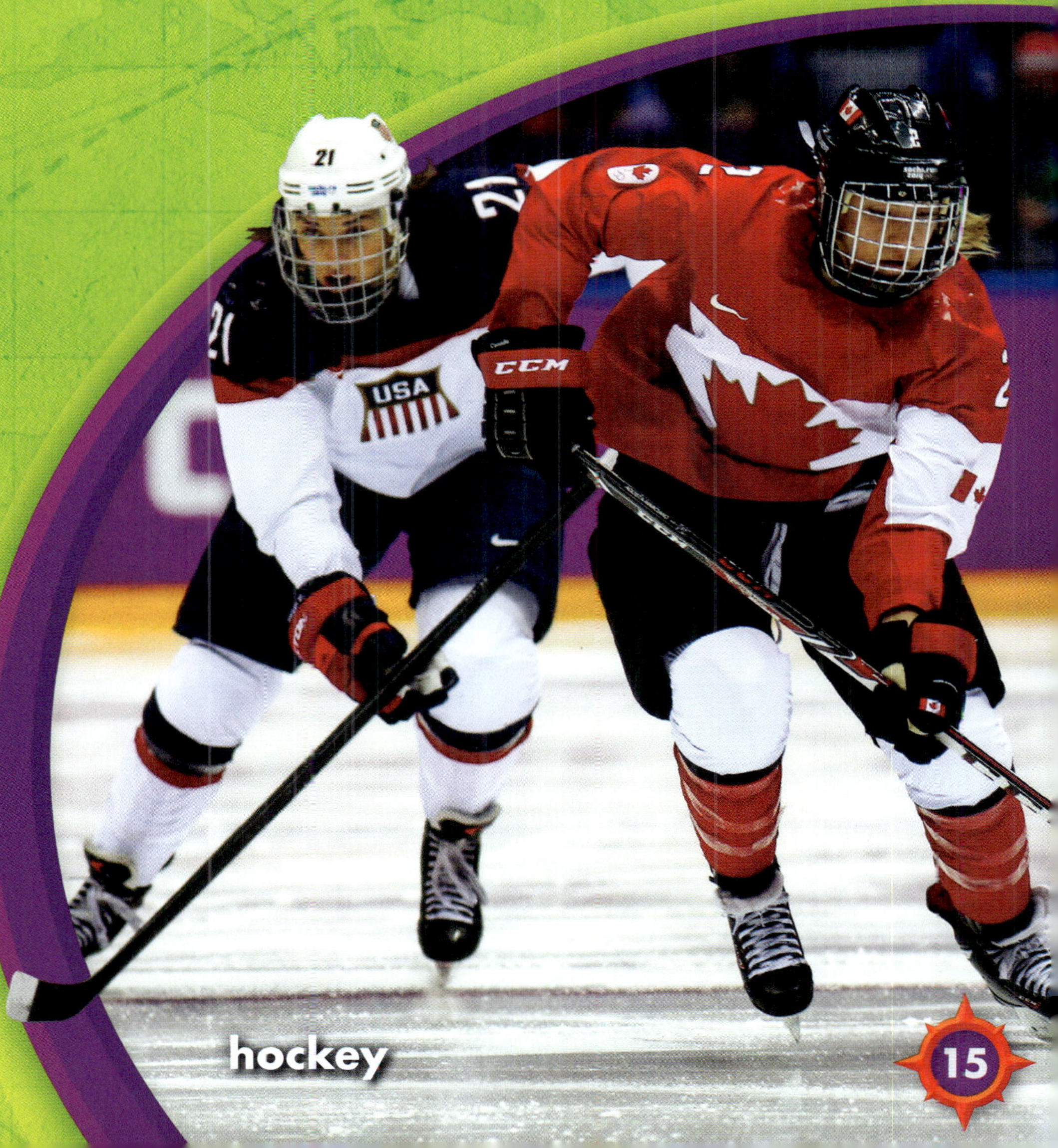

hockey

15

Poutine is a famous Canadian dish. It is fries with cheese and gravy. Split pea soup is also popular.

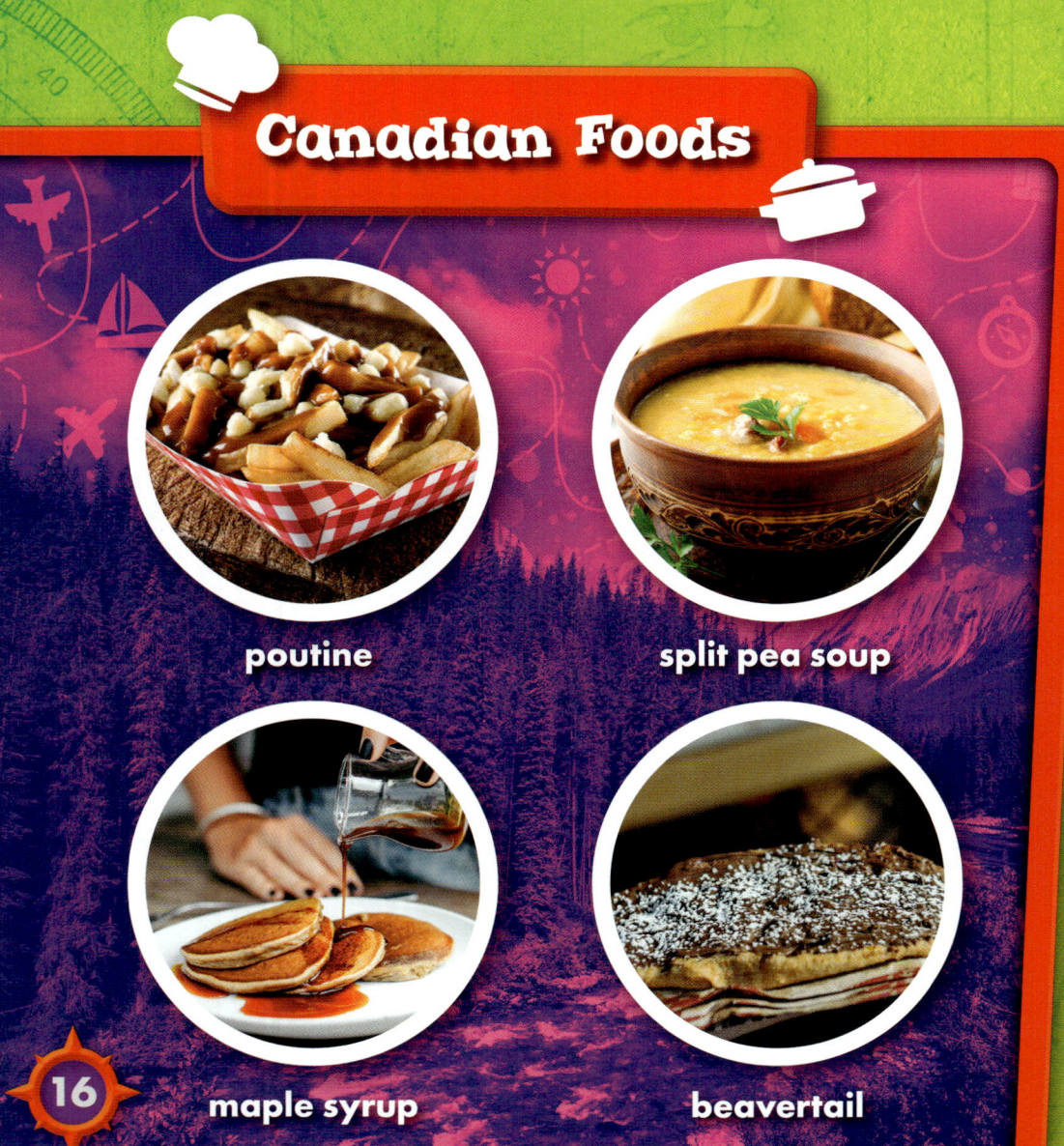

Canadian Foods

poutine

split pea soup

maple syrup

beavertail

children eating maple syrup

Maple syrup is a sweet topping. Beavertails are tasty treats!

Canada Day

Canada has many fun holidays. Canada Day is July 1. Canadians watch parades and fireworks.

Many enjoy Boxing Day on December 26. There are many things to **celebrate** in Canada!

Canada Facts

Size:
3,855,103 square miles
(9,984,670 square kilometers)

Population:
38,232,593 (2022)

National Holiday:
Canada Day (July 1)

Main Languages:
English, French

Capital City:
Ottawa

Famous Face

Name: Sandra Oh

Famous For: a famous actor in movies such as *Turning Red*

Religions

- none: 24%
- other: 9%
- Catholic: 39%
- other Christian: 28%

Top Landmarks

Canadian Rockies

Lake Louise

Niagara Falls

Glossary

Arctic—the area near the North Pole

celebrate—to do something special or fun for a big event, occasion, or holiday

cultures—customs and beliefs of certain groups of people

curling—a game in which two teams of four players slide stones on ice toward a target

graze—to eat grass or other plants growing in a field

plains—large areas of flat land

population—the total number of people who live in a certain place

range—a group of mountains

wander—to move around without a specific direction

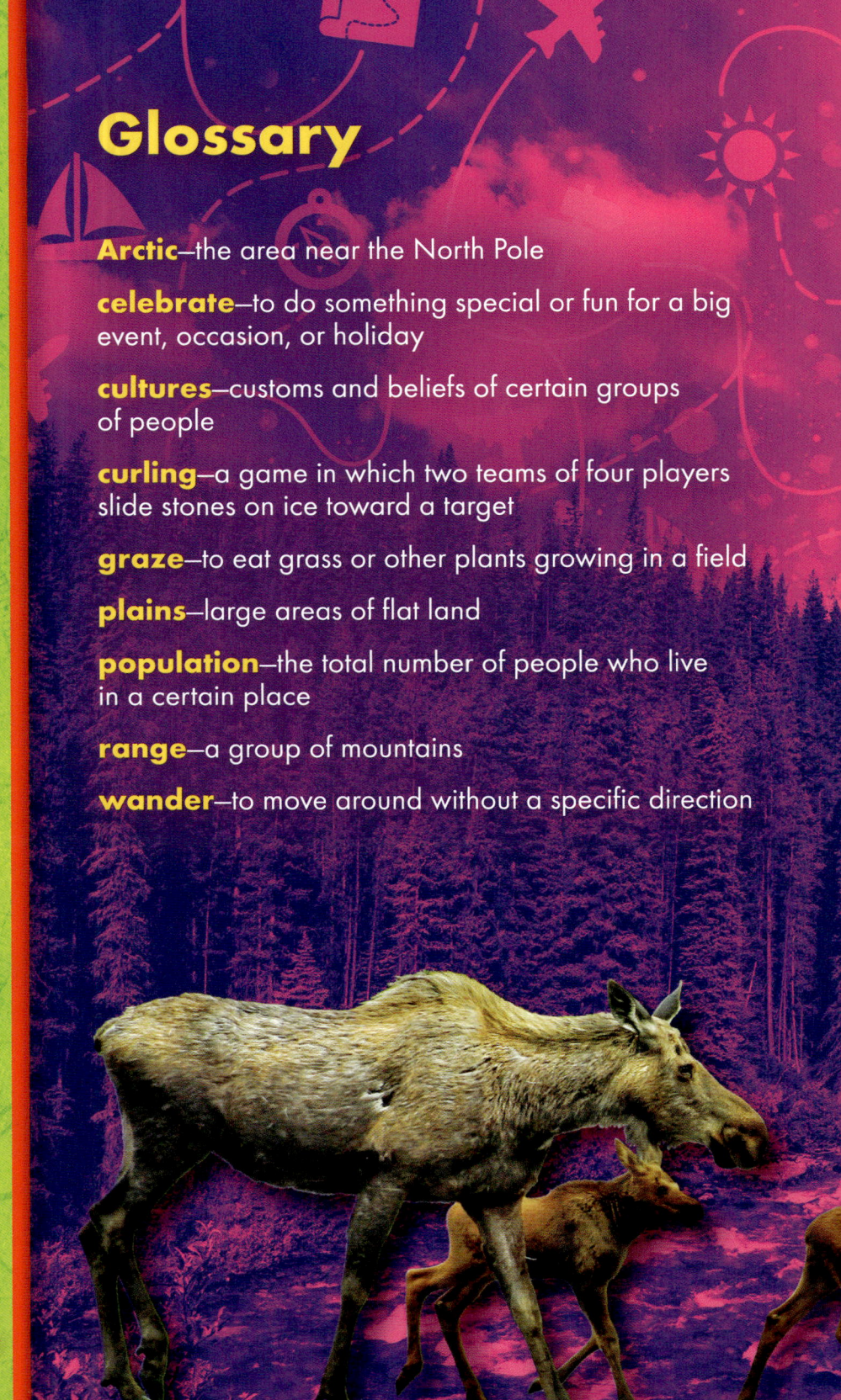

To Learn More

AT THE LIBRARY

Dean, Jessica. *Canada*. Minneapolis, Minn.: Pogo, 2019.

Frisch-Schmoll, Joy. *Let's Look at Canada*. North Mankato, Minn.: Capstone Press, 2019.

Lin, Chelsea. *Weird but True! Canada: 300 Outrageous Facts about the True North*. Washington, D.C.: National Geographic, 2018.

ON THE WEB

FACTSURFER

Factsurfer.com gives you a safe, fun way to find more information.

1. Go to www.factsurfer.com.
2. Enter "Canada" into the search box and click 🔍.
3. Select your book cover to see a list of related content.

Index

animals, 10, 11
Arctic, 8, 11
Boxing Day, 19
Canada Day, 18
Canada facts, 20-21
Canadian Rockies, 8, 9
Canadian Shield, 6
canoeing, 14
capital (see Ottawa)
cities, 12
curling, 14
downhill skiing, 14
English, 12
foods, 16, 17
French, 12, 13
hockey, 15
lakes, 6
map, 5

North America, 5
Ottawa, 4, 5
people, 12
plains, 7, 11
say hello, 13
size, 4
Toronto, 12

The images in this book are reproduced through the courtesy of: Gilberto Mesquita, front cover; BGSmith, front cover, p. 21 (Lake Louise); Pamela MacNaughtan, pp. 2-3; Vitelle, p. 3; valleyboi63, pp. 4-5; Vlad G, p. 5; Marc Filion, pp. 6-7; Dancestrokes, p. 7; Derek Robbins, p. 8; Kabindra shrestha, pp. 8-9; Real Window Creative, pp. 10-11; Dennis Stogsdill, p. 11 (moose); Mark Caunt, p. 11 (black bear); Adam Cegledi, p. 11 (bison); Jim Cumming, p. 11 (snowy owl); Richard Cavalleri, pp. 12, 18-19; Marina Poushkina, pp. 12-13; fokke baarssen, pp. 14-15; nojustice, p. 14 (inset); Iurii Osadchi, p. 15; Foodio, p. 16 (poutine); nesavinov, p. 16 (split pea soup); Sveta Y, p. 16 (maple syrup); David Giral/ Alamy, p. 16 (beavertail); lisegagne, p. 17; titoOnz, p. 20 (flag); Kathy Hutchins, p. 20 (Sandra Oh); Harry Beugelink, p. 21 (Canadian Rockies); Igor Sh, p. 21 (Niagra Falls); Amanda Wayne, pp. 22-23.